Bootstrapping A Lawn Care Business

by LN Marks

Foreword

Building a lawn care business does not have to be hard. It does not have to cost a lot of money. In fact, you can start off without spending a single penny or taking on any debt. It is called bootstrapping, and it is what this short guide will teach.

Oxford Languages defines the verb bootstrap as follows:

<u>Get (oneself or something) into or out of a situation using existing resources.</u>

Did you read that and wonder what resources you have that will get you started in the lawn care business? If so, then starting at Chapter 1 is for you. You do not need a single thing to get started other than a desire to work.

If you already have some tools and equipment, you can skip ahead. But this is a short read, and you might learn something. So, I encourage you to just read the whole thing. It should not take more than one hour of your time.

Now is an important time for a disclaimer:

This guide will not teach you how to win contracts.

This guide will not teach you how to compete directly with major companies.

This is not a comprehensive guide, but instead a set of specific ideas meant to get you started.

This guide will teach you how to fit into your market one customer at a time.

There is no guarantee of performance. I wish that I could promise success, but a lot of it depends on you.

You are responsible for educating yourself on relevant laws, ordinances, safety procedures, etc. This guide will not cover any of those especially important items.

Now that we have that out of the way, turn the page and we will get started teaching you how to bootstrap your way into a lawn care business.

Contents

Chapter 1: Getting Started With Nothing

1.1. What Is The Plan?

So, you want to start a lawn care business. Great! But you do not own any tools or equipment necessary for a lawn care business. That is OKAY! You do not need to buy anything. We are going to find your first customer anyway.

To get started, take a walk around your neighborhood. Do not drive. Gas and vehicle maintenance cost too much money, and we are starting this business with NOTHING. So, take a walk around your neighborhood. Look for lawns that are not well maintained. Make a list. These are potential customers. Do not do anything more than make a list today. Ideally you will walk until you have identified 20 lawns that do not appear to get regular attention.

In addition to unkempt lawns, you should also look at other yard related issues. Are there bushes in the yard? If so, do they look neatly trimmed, or are they growing wild? Are there leaves that appear to have been collecting all season? Is the driveway dirty and stained? Make notes on all of these things. Most important, see if any of these houses have lawn equipment visible. If you see a lawnmower, a leaf blower, or a pressure washer at a house with a lawn care deficit, make a big note about it.

When you get home, study these notes. Put the houses in order of who might be most likely to hire you to attend to their lawn care needs. Start with any house that appears to already have equipment. Get your list and get ready to work!

1.2. Making The Ask

You are at your first house. This could be your first customer. You are impeccably dressed, but in work clothes. First impressions make all the difference. Do not ever approach a customer for the first time if you are dirty or look unkempt. Be sure your shirt is tucked in. Smile. Do not put your hands in your pockets. Always keep your hands where customers can see them.

Knock on the door or ring the doorbell. Then take a step back. You are still smiling, right? When someone answers the door, introduce yourself. Explain that you are looking to do yard work. Tell them that you do not have your own equipment yet, but you would be happy to mow their lawn with their lawn mower. Tell them the first mow is discounted, it will only be $15.00 for the front yard and $15.00 for the back yard. Offer to trim any bushes that need it if they have clippers or trimmers. $5.00 per bush. Do they have a leaf blower and need the driveway blown off? $5.00. Do they have a pressure washer and want their driveway pressure washed? $20.00.

The point here is to find something that they could probably do themselves, with equipment they already have. Then offer them a deal for you to do it for them, with their equipment. If you are a good salesperson, and if you have a little bit of luck, your first house might take you up on the offer. That would be awesome! You need a plan in place for either scenario. What will you do if they agree, and what will you do if they say, "No, thank you." Plan this out ahead of time so that you look prepared and professional.

1.2.1. If They Say Yes

This is easy. If they are interested, do whatever jobs they are willing to pay you for. Take your time and do an excellent job. You want them to be impressed, because you want to come back next week and charge them full price. Be sure to discard any clippings and trimmings exactly where and how they tell you to. Be incredibly careful with the equipment you are borrowing.

A note on equipment: always ask them if there is anything unusual about their equipment. Check the oil. Take a look at blades to make sure they are in good condition. And never under any circumstances should you attempt to use a piece of equipment or machinery unless you are completely familiar with proper safe operating procedures. If you do not know how to use something, then do not risk it. It is not worth possibly hurting yourself or someone else. It is not worth the potential hassle of having to replace something you broke.

Once you have finished the work and collected payment, go home. That is right, go home. You need to make sure you still look presentable before going to your next potential customer. If that means a shower and a change of clothes, then that is what it means. After you have established a regular book of business, it will be okay to go from job to job without cleaning up in between. But remember: never ever knock on a door for the first time if you do not look your absolute best.

1.2.2. If They Say No

If they say no, thank them politely and move on. Do not ask follow-up questions, and certainly do not attempt to cajole and convince. That time will be better spent getting to the next house and finding someone who wants to say yes.

Even if you are always polite, you will occasionally run across a grumpy individual. This person might be chronically unhappy, or just having a bad day, but they decide to take it out on you. Do not push back, do not argue. Thank them for their time, keep your smile in place, and move on. Trust me, it is the best thing you can do.

If you are polite, there is a possibility that the person who says no will offer a suggestion for someone who might be interested in what you are offering. Always remember to say thank you.

Professionalism goes a long way, and part of being professional is appropriately handling people who do not want to work with you.

Chapter 2: Building Your Business

2.1. Money!

You have finished with your first customer and gotten paid. Remember, this is not your personal money. This is money for your business. You need to keep careful track of this, and do not mix business money with personal money. To start with, you can track your income and expenses (you should not have expenses yet!) in a simple spreadsheet. It can even be a pen and paper spreadsheet.

Find a local bank that wants your business. Learn what their minimums are to open an account. Ideally you want two accounts. It is perfectly fine to open an account in your name and operate your business under a dba (doing business as). If you tell your banker this is what you want to do, they will be able to set it up.

The first account you want is your main account. This is where you will deposit everything you earn. Remember, it is only used for business. Do not buy groceries, or snacks, or anything else that is not 100% business related out of this account.

The second account you want is for taxes. Any time you pay yourself money out of the main account, you need to put money aside for taxes. Look at last year's return. What percentage of your income did you pay in taxes? That is what you should set aside. This way, when taxes are due next year, you will not have any nasty surprises. Any extra tax you owe because of your new side hustle will be sitting in the tax account, ready and waiting.

A note on taxes: if your income from your lawn care business grows to be more than about 15% of your total income, it is time to talk to a tax professional about how to structure your business. The advice above is good for small side-hustle amounts of money, not for serious income. If your lawn care business becomes your primary source of income, you absolutely must discuss your business with a tax professional, preferably a certified public accountant.

2.2. Buying Equipment

Once you have some money in your account, you can start looking at buying equipment. There are several things to consider when deciding what to buy.

2.2.1. Will It Fit?

If you are driving a two-seat sports car, do not buy a lawn mower unless you intend to walk it everywhere you go. Too many people in lawn care justify needing a newer, bigger, fancier vehicle (often a truck) to haul their equipment around. You do not have fancy truck money yet. You barely have lawn mower money.

Remember, we are bootstrapping this business. That means paying cash for everything. No borrowing money.

So, the first thing to consider when you are ready to buy equipment is if it will fit in your current vehicle. This may sound ridiculous. It is based on experience. Many people have gotten into debt because they did not start with this question in mind.

2.2.2. Do I Need It?

Has anyone expressed interest in having you pressure wash their driveway? If not, then do not buy a pressure washer. If you only have one single customer who pays you to pressure wash their driveway, and they only need it once per year, do not buy a pressure washer.

This exact same theory applies to anything you buy. Buy items that you know you need because you already borrow them from multiple customers. One of the most dangerous thoughts you can have is, "If I had this, I'm sure it would pay for itself in no time." Think through purchases carefully and have a plan.

If you find a customer who wants you to do something for them, but neither you nor they have the equipment, then rent what you need. Charge the customer enough to cover the rental and still maintain the profits you want. And then if you find yourself renting the same tool or machine repeatedly, consider buying it. But make sure the cost adds up. A good rule of thumb is that if you spend enough on rentals in a month that you could have bought one, it is probably time to buy one. Stated another way: Do not buy something just because you had to rent it once.

2.2.3. Can I Maintain It?

If you are going to build a successful business and own your own equipment, it needs to be well cared for. Buy equipment that is easy to keep in good working order, and then do the work to keep it in good working order.

This also means that when you are looking at a piece of equipment, make sure it does not require special care. You want all of your equipment to take roughly the same gasoline, oil, and 2-cycle ratios. Otherwise, you will have to keep multiple fuel cans, or risk damaging something.

Be certain to educate yourself on proper maintenance for everything you own for your business. Learning to repair broken items yourself is also a valuable use of time.

As with all tools and machines, be absolutely certain that you know and are implementing safe use practices at all times. Do not use equipment you are not familiar with. Do not ever attempt to repair a machine if you are not familiar with proper procedures.

2.2.4. Where Will I Keep It?

A major aspect of equipment maintenance is proper storage. If all of your tools and equipment stay outside, they will not last long at all. But you cannot keep them in your bedroom, either. Be sure you have a safe place to properly store anything you buy BEFORE you buy it.

This may sound like common sense, but many people skip this step when making purchases. If you do not have proper storage available, then you need to commit to continuing to rent that particular piece of equipment until you can afford storage. Storage may mean adding a shed in your back yard, or it may mean renting a storage unit. If you have to store your equipment somewhere other than your house, factor in travel time when calculating expenses.

2.2.5. Buy Used

For any purchase, consider buying the item used. You want good quality, but low price. Repair shops will often sell unclaimed items for the repair price owed on them. Pawn shops often have high quality, gently used items. Be aware of the cost of new; many pawn shops will overcharge significantly for items. Thrift and discount stores also occasionally have items you are looking for.

Be mindful when looking for deals. Only buy what you walked into an establishment intending to buy. You do not make enough money to buy something on whim, even if the price is fantastic. Have a plan and stick to it. That is the key to being successful long-term.

2.3. Updating Pricing

Your first customers got good discounts because you were only giving them your time and energy. They provided the equipment. Now you are also creating wear and tear on equipment you own. Your prices need to account for this.

Now is the time to really begin to carve out your niche. Remember, you are building a successful business without going into debt. You are not trying to compete against big companies.

In almost every town there is a set of customers that the big companies ignore. These customers are not looking for fancy lawn service. They do not want chemical treatments. They do not have a lot of money to pay. They just do not want to get a code violation for having their yard look unkempt.

The best niche for starting out is to cater to this target customer. You want a reasonable price that does not include a lot of extras. For $20.00 - $30.00 you will mow their front yard. Give a small reduction to add the back yard, unless it is substantially larger. Once you have the equipment, offer edging, leaf blowing, bush trimming, and other ancillary services as optional add-ons. But your base offering is a quick, quality cut on the front yard.

Do not spend a lot of time on selling additional services unless there is an obvious need. Are the bushes growing taller than the house? Okay, recommend a trim. Is the grass creeping into the driveway? It is perfectly reasonable to offer edging. But in order to differentiate yourself, you have to focus on the simple value you can offer that your larger competitors treat as "not worth it."

Just remember to keep track of your expenses. Remember that your time is very valuable and be certain you are tracking it as well. For every customer you should be able to determine what your job profit was. You need to have a formula in place that tells you how much of that profit you will pay yourself. It should not be all of the profit. You want to keep some money inside of the business for maintenance and new equipment.

If you find that a job was not profitable, you need to quickly examine the reasons. Did it take longer than usual? Did you make a mistake in pricing it? Whatever the reason, first look for ways to make the job profitable next time without raising prices. If that is not possible, then you will need to talk to the customer about a price increase.

2.4. Your First Company Truck

Up to this point you have been hauling equipment in your personal vehicle. Now, you need a dedicated company vehicle. You may even need a trailer to go with it. Be careful - this step is where most people screw up everything they have been working for. You do not want to be most people.

First things first: be sure you have somewhere to store it. We covered this earlier, when discussing buying equipment. Well, your company vehicle and trailer are equipment. If you do not have a safe, secure storage area, then it is not time to make this purchase.

Do not even think about going to a dealer. You do not have dealer money. Stop it. You are bootstrapping, and a dealer is going to oversell you into a car note. A car note means you will not earn a profit. You need to find a good quality, used vehicle. No new trailer, either. Someone is always selling a trailer they do not need any more. You may have to do some looking around, and you may not get everything you need in one day. But that is not a problem.

Buy something appropriate. Not too big, not too small. Do not buy something unusual. You need a reliable vehicle that is easy to keep running. Make sure the engine, transmission, and chassis are all rated to comfortably haul all of the equipment you will carry.

If you struggle with negotiating, do not put yourself into a high-pressure sales situation. You will buy more truck than you need. The best tactic in this situation is to complete your test drive and handle the negotiation over the phone. Whether it is a new car (it should not be - get off that new car lot!) or used, the salesman has been trained in how to read your body language and knows what to say to get you to sign the order. So, take away his advantage. Call in to negotiate. If you feel uncomfortable, hang up. Call back once you have calmed back down.

2.5. Insurance

Very early in your lawn care business you should talk to an insurance agent about appropriate types and levels of insurance to carry. Any time you add a service, or piece of equipment, or employee, update them. It is important to protect yourself, and you should not skip this step.

Chapter 3: Growing Your Business

3.1. Growing Pains

If you are good, you will eventually have more customers than you can comfortably service in your available time. At this point you will be forced to make a decision. How will you move your business forward?

3.1.1. Quit Growing

Once you have a full schedule, you can just stop taking new customers. If you are comfortable with the money you are earning, this is not necessarily a bad decision. Just remember that sometimes customers quit using you. Their financial situation could change. They might move. Their child may now be old enough that they make the lawn a weekly chore. If you decide to stop adding customers, just be prepared to go back into sales mode if you lose a customer.

If you do decide to quit growing, you should find a friendly competitor who might be willing to take the customer on. Set up an agreement so you get a referral fee. This way you can still make a little money even if you do not pick up the customer. Just be sure that anyone you refer will do a good job, because your referral will reflect on you and your business.

This can be a tough decision to make, especially if you have an entrepreneurial mindset. The urge to "grow, grow, grow" can be very strong. Understand that it is okay to level out if the money you are making is at a comfortable level. There is no shame is maintaining a steady level of business.

And the decision to stop adding new customers does not have to be permanent. That is the great thing about the lawn care business. You can decide to pause your growth for a while, then decide later to start growing again. Being flexible means you have many options.

3.1.2. Replace Low-Margin Customers

Another option when your schedule becomes full is to replace customers who are not the most profitable. Maybe they have an odd yard, and it takes you twice as long to do the work. Maybe you took on a customer in an outlying neighborhood when you were trying to build your lawn care business, but now they are too far out of the way. If you are keeping track of profitability, low-margin customers will be easy to identify. Replacing them with customers who allow you to earn more money in the same amount of time is a reasonable thing to do.

This is another situation where you want to have someone ready to pick up the customer and pay you a referral fee for the privilege. Again, remember that anyone you refer is a reflection on you and your lawn care business, so do not make referrals unless you know the person will do a good job.

3.1.3. Hire An Employee

The thought of hiring an employee can be overwhelming. Now someone is relying on you for their paycheck. And depending on how your customer pay, now you might have someone handling your cash. It is a huge decision, and it is one that you should think about very carefully.

When you first add an employee, your income will shrink. There is no way to avoid it. The idea is that you are able to quickly add more customers. After a month or two, your income should be back where it was before you added an employee. After another month you should be making more money than ever before.

If you have never managed an employee before you need to learn how. Read several books on leadership and management. Be picky with who you hire. Have clear expectations and enforce them. Do not tolerate a poor employee. If you have problems, fire them as quickly as possible.

Do not over-extend yourself too quickly. If something happens you need to be able to handle your customers without interruption. Remember that life happens. Your employee might call in sick, or quit. You might have to fire them. Be prepared for any of these scenarios.

After you have hired an employee, go back to your first steps of knocking on doors. If you have some money set aside (and you should if you have been paying attention!) you might consider advertising. You can repeat this cycle and eventually end up with multiple teams of employees completing hundreds of jobs every week.

3.2. Advertising & Marketing

If you decide to engage in marketing, there are many methods to choose from. You do not have to pick just one. Do not put a large amount of money into any single strategy until you know it works. Here we will go over several options. This is not a comprehensive list.

Please keep the following in mind with any form of advertising. You want potential customers to contact you, so you need a method that allows them to do this. They will expect to receive your response promptly. Do not engage in marketing if you are not prepared to handle the inquiries you receive. You will just be wasting money, making people mad, and ruining your business reputation. Start small. You can always go back and go bigger.

Another consideration is the quality of your advertising. Have someone proofread everything. Make sure you are spelling words correctly and have no typos. Make sure your advertising is easy to read. Do not get too fancy. Keep it clean and simple. Your advertising is a direct reflection on your business, and your business is making lawns look clean and simple, right?

Finally, try different variations. If you are doing this correctly and starting small, you can test many different ideas. When you find something that works well you can increase that one. Everything you are doing is about taking one small step at a time. If you do this, it will be much harder to make a business-killing mistake.

3.2.1. Referrals

Your existing customers can be your best source for new customers. Offer a discount for referrals. Be sure to ask for referrals politely, but do not be afraid to ask. You can even put something in writing. A really good method of incentivizing referrals is to offer a discount to both your existing customer and the new customer. A twist on this is to make the discounts valid for the <u>second</u> service. That way you get a full-price service and a return trip for the discount.

3.2.2. Print Advertising

Many lawn care businesses send out fancy flyers in the mail. This is expensive, and the percentage of customers you gain versus flyers mailed is often ridiculously small. If you decide to give this a try, be sure you can target neighborhoods where the flyers will be delivered.

Another popular method is hand-delivery of printed flyers. Be absolutely certain you are not creating litter. Also know the laws around where you can deliver; some neighborhoods and municipalities do not allow this.

3.2.3. Online Advertising

Social media is great for advertising. You can determine who your ideal customer is and target your ads. Start small. A little can often go a long way with an effective online ad. You want to be able to handle the volume of inquiries.

3.3. The Off Season

The lawn care business is definitely a seasonal business. You need a strategy for maintaining income, especially if you have employees.

If you decide to only operate your lawn care business seasonally, be sure your employees know that when you hire them. Also be sure your customers are aware. Ask them if they have needs you can handle.

If you do stay operational during the off season, you need a service to offer that adds value for your customers. Depending on your location, this could be snow-related. Perhaps there are leaves that still need to be raked/blown. There are many lawn maintenance chores that are best done during the winter months.

You can also branch out. One service that you can offer to existing customers is to help with exterior holiday decorations. Haul boxes out of storage, hang exterior lights, set up lawn decorations. This service is especially popular with older customers who want the joy of having decorations but may no longer be physically capable of decorating like they used to.

Be careful when handling decorations. Be especially carefully when stringing lights together. Improperly strung lights are a potential fire hazard. Follow all safety procedures.

3.4. Exit Strategy

Always be thinking about your exit strategy. Manage everything like you plan on listing your lawn care business for sale tomorrow. Keep your books clean. That means report all income no matter what, and never mix personal and business money. Always pay yourself and be very clear about how much you are paying yourself.

If you build the business properly and have clean books, you will be able to sell it for a comfortable profit. Your sales price should be the value of your equipment, and some multiple of your annual profits. Different areas command different multiples. If you need to sell quickly, consider starting at a 3x multiple. That means you would list the business for sale at 3 times your annual profit, plus the value of your equipment.

You started this business from the ground up with no money, but plenty of people buy existing businesses. If you can prove your income and demonstrate consistency of customer accounts, someone will be happy to buy from you.

Do not offer any owner financing. If you are getting out, get out. You have no control over how well a buyer will run what used to be your business. If they lose all of the customers, they cannot pay what they owe you. Get all of your money up front.

3.5. Conclusion

So, there it is. In less than an hour you have learned how to get started in the lawn care business without incurring debt or spending any money. What will you do with this knowledge? Hopefully your next step is to grab a pen and paper, put on your shoes, and go take a walk around your neighborhood!